THE SUNKEN KEEP

THE SUNKEN KEEP

A version of Giuseppe Ungaretti's *Il Porto Sepolto*

ANDREW FITZSIMONS

Drawings by Sergio Maria Calatroni

ISOBAR PRESS

First published in 2017 by

Isobar Press
Sakura 2-21-23-202, Setagaya-ku
Tokyo 156-0053, Japan
&
14 Isokon Flats, Lawn Road
London NW3 2XD, United Kingdom

http://isobarpress.com

ISBN 978-4-907359-22-5

ACKNOWLEDGEMENTS

The Italian text used for this version is that of the 1916 first
edition, re-published as: Giuseppe Ungaretti, *Il Porto Sepolto*,
ed. Carlo Ossola (Venezia: Marsilio Editori, 1990).

Contents

NOTE: *In the introduction, names of Japanese writers are given in the Japanese order, with the family name first. All translations from the Italian or French are by Andrew Fitzsimons.*

INTRODUCTION

The word never reveals the secret that is in us but we close in on it.

Giuseppe Ungaretti

Il Porto Sepolto was written between December 1915 and October 1916 in the trenches of the Carso plateau in Friuli while Giuseppe Ungaretti was serving as a private in the 19th Infantry, Brescia Brigade, of the Italian army. For Ungaretti the writing was an examination of self, he said, carried out day by day on whatever scrap of paper was to hand: the margins of old newspapers; the white spaces in letters received; stuffed away then into his backpack. The poems were a form of company and succour, with little thought for a public. As Mark Thompson recounts in *The White War: Life and Death on the Italian Front 1915–1919* (Faber, 2008), the poems owed their publication to a chance encounter with a literary-minded lieutenant, Ettore Serra, to whom the last piece is addressed. Passing through the town of Versa, where the 19th Infantry were resting,

> [h]is eye was caught by a ragged, insouciant soldier who was taking such pleasure in the sunshine that he failed to salute the passing officer. Serra wanted his name, which led to a conversation about a few early poems that Ungaretti had published in a magazine. Asked about his recent work, Ungaretti dug in his pockets for the scraps of paper. Serra took them away and turned them into a book that changed Italian poetry.

The poems were published at Udine in an edition of eighty copies in December 1916. A revised version with the same title went on to form the second part of Ungaretti's *Allegria di Naufragi* (1919). The present translation is of that first Udine edition republished in 1990 (Venezia: Marsilio Editori) edited by Carlo Ossola.

As Thompson indicates, these thirty poems are central to Ungaretti's revitalizing of Italian poetic language; a renovation of rhythm, syntax, punctuation and diction comparable to the impact on English poetry of T. S. Eliot and Ezra Pound, and comparable also to the work of William Carlos Williams, given the resemblance between how both poets set about reconfiguring the parameters of the poetic line in their respective traditions, as well as their commitment to 'particulars.'

As central as the book is to Italian poetry in the twentieth century, it also holds a unique place in Ungaretti's poetry. It was not only his first collection but, as Carlo Ossola has written, the point of origin for Ungaretti's personal myth of exodus and journey toward a promised land. The imagery of this journey – the desert, the wanderings and dreams of the nomad, light as both gift and curse – owed much to the circumstances of his birth and upbringing. He was born in Alexandria, Egypt, in 1888, to parents with Tuscan origins. His father, a labourer on the Suez Canal, was killed in a work accident when Ungaretti was two. His mother supported the family by running a bakery, on the edge of the desert. Ungaretti, like many of the Italian community in Egypt, was raised bilingually in French, and attended French schools in Alexandria. In 1912 he moved to Paris and became involved in the rich cultural life of the city, attended lectures by Bergson, and befriended, among others, Braque, De Chirico, Modigliani, Picasso, and the poets Blaise Cendrars and Guillaume Apollinaire, both of whom were strong influences on his poetry – the journal-like dating and naming of place at the end of each poem in *Il Porto Sepolto* owes something to Cendrars, for instance, and traces of Apollinaire's *poèmes-conversations* (talk poems) can be found in the introductory poem written in memory of the friend of his youth, Mohammed Sceab. At the outbreak of World War I, Ungaretti moved to Italy for the first time, and in 1915 volunteered for service in the Italian army.

In this same year Ungaretti's first poems appeared in *Lacerba*, a journal founded in 1913 in Florence by Giovanni Papini and Ardengo Soffici. Some of the poems that eventually appeared in *Il Porto Sepolto* were first published in 1916 in the journal *La Diana*, edited by his friend Gherardo Marone. Whether Ungaretti in *Il Porto Sepolto* was working under the influence of Japanese poetry is a matter of some debate, but he had certainly encountered the work of Japanese poets in Italian translation in *La Diana*, his own poem 'Fase' ('Phase') having appeared in issue number 5 (May 1916), on the page immediately following translations of tanka poems by Yosano Akiko. Marone collected his *La Diana* translations, which he had begun in 1915 in collaboration with Shimoi Harukichi, a Japanese fascist fellow-traveller teaching at the Regio Istituto Orientale in Naples, in a volume entitled *Poesie giapponesi* (Naples, Ricciardi, 1917). (Ungaretti himself, much to his later embarrassment, had sympathized with the fascist movement in its early days, and Mussolini even wrote a perfunctory introduction to the second edition of *Il Porto Sepolto*, published in 1923.)

Poesie giapponesi featured not only Yosano Akiko, but the tanka poetry of Maeda Sumitaka (transcribed as 'Suikei Maeta'), Yosano Tekkan, Sasaki Nobutsuna and Yoshii Isamu. In the spring of 1917, Ungaretti wrote to Marone from the front requesting a copy of the anthology. At the 1979 International Ungaretti Conference at Urbino, Suga Atsuko argued that Ungaretti's knowledge of Japanese poetry was limited to these poets and that he could not have had knowledge of haiku. Nevertheless, a sharpening of Ungaretti's style is evident between the poems published in *Lacerba* in 1915 and those published the following year in *La Diana*, and the 'family resemblance' to haiku in 'Finestra a Mare' ('Window on the Sea,' p. 31) is remarkable:

Balaustrata di brezza
per appoggiare la mia malinconia
stasera

Breezeblown balustrade
to take the weight of my melancholy
this evening

Marone's discussion of Ungaretti in an essay in his *Difesa di Dulcinea* (1920) is filled with excitement at the discovery of a poet who fulfills the qualities he found in Japanese poetry: in *Il Porto Sepolto* he says, 'a few words are enough to convey to us the marvelous spectacle of nature,' quoting 'Finestra a Mare,' and 'Tramonto' ('Sunset,' p. 30):

Il carnato di cielo
sveglia oasi
al nomade d'amore

The fleshtoned sky
awakens oases
in the nomad of love

Here is poetry, Marone says, reduced to essential notation, in lines with an assured lightness of touch: 'for the first time in Italy we are in the presence of a noble attempt at classical poetry in the pure sense of the word.' What Marone meant by 'classical' echoes his ideas about Japanese poetry: 'supreme refinement of that which adds to life, pure and free of every extraneous element in its extreme essentiality; life's elemental and spiritual form; a genuine adhesion to the world of things.' The value of Japanese poetry resides in all genuine poetry, he argues, 'in the particular raised to the universal ... in the moment become infinite.' It is in this sense that Ungaretti is for Marone 'Japanese.' Quoting the last tercet of 'Lindoro di Deserto' ('Lindoro of the Desert,' p. 23), he writes: 'the sense of vastness and distance is rendered so profoundly and so impalpably that we search in vain to discover the secret among the elementary words: everything is suspended over a pause, in equilibrium between two silences.' Marone's reading of Ungaretti is informed, of course, by knowledge of the *kireji*, the 'cutting word' of haiku, and awareness of that form's juxtaposition of two (almost) independent images. Yet it is well to recall that there were other currents contributing to this element in Ungaretti, not least the French artistic milieu. As Joseph Cary has written, Ungaretti liked to quote with approval the following words of his contemporary, Pierre Reverdy:

> The image is a pure creation of the intelligence. It cannot be born of a comparison but from the bringing together of two more or less widely separated realities. The more the rapports between the two realities brought together are mutually distant and at the same time precise (*lointains et justes*), the stronger the image will be, the more it will possess of emotive power and poetic reality…

In a 1958 paper on Ungaretti's informing influences, alongside Japan, Oreste Macrí noted the importance of Arabic songs and literature ('the chant / of the Koran / over coffee,' p. 19), as well as popular song, but awarded 'pre-eminence' to the Paris years in the 'school of Apollinaire.'

If the specifics of the Japanese influence on *Il Porto Sepolto* are a matter of debate, the resemblance in form was noted from the very moment of publication, in 1917, when the brevity of the poems caused Marone himself to first invoke the comparison. Giovanni Papini and Elpidio Jenco in the same year made similar claims, significant for – if little else – a peculiar confounding of *chinoiserie* and *japonisme*, and Jenco's comparison of Ungaretti to Sasaki Nobutsuna for his 'desire to harmonize with the infinite.' As Anna Lisa Somma has shown, Ungaretti, at this time, did not reject such comparisons, partly because the novelty and literary acclaim Japanese poetry was receiving in Italy was helping to make his own work and name more known. Yet Ungaretti's feelings changed and resentment at the comparison began to

appear in his letters and comments from the 1920s on. In a letter
of 1929, his frustration is palpable:

> This is how it is: during the war, in the trenches, I
> wrote a poetic diary: notes in poetic form, metaphysical
> impressions, screams from the soul, short, rapidly, since
> in those days, for whoever was in combat, eternity
> was one moment. In that period, I sent these prayers
> of mine to a literary magazine in Naples, *La Diana*.
> Destiny wanted it that in those days the editor of *La
> Diana*, Gherardo Marone, who didn't know a word of
> Japanese, should get together with a Japanese who knew
> little Italian, to translate Japanese poets. Young people
> at that time were under my influence and it happened
> that the rhythms, and diction, in Marone's translations,
> were those of my work. From then on there hasn't been
> a critic, anthologist, even foreign ones, who, speaking of
> me, doesn't mention Japan[.]

And despite his disavowals, the connection continues to be
made. The great contemporary Italian poet Andrea Zanzotto in
his preface to *Cento Haiku* (1982) qualified, even as he repeated,
the claim, 'One might wonder whether the unmistakable aura
of early Ungaretti was not affected by, in ways more or less
subterranean, the suggestions of haiku, so impressive at times is
the similarity of their formal shapes.' What Ungaretti found, at
the very least, in the Japanese poetry that he had undoubtedly
read, was a confirmation of what he privileged in his own
poems: the essential word, a poetry of the noun and naming
in reaction against the poetry of contemporaries in the school
of what he called the 'oh and ah' and 'adjectives,' a poetry of
spontaneous address to pressing occasion. The encounter with
Japanese poetry corroborated the poems he was writing in the
trenches, and confirmed him in a practice that led to such an
extraordinary poem as 'Soldati' ('Soldiers'):

Abide
as in autumn
on trees
the leaves

Ungaretti out-does the brevity of haiku with his most famous
poem, 'Mattina' ('Morning'), seven syllables short:

M'illumino
d'immenso

To render this in English is a thankless task, so specifically does it
live within the possibilities of the Italian language. One possible
literalizing: 'I illuminate myself with the immense.' Another:
'Be-lighted / by th'immense.' Or what about Yeats's 'riddled with
light' ('The Cold Heaven')? Ungaretti's seven syllables emerge
out of Leopardi's 'L'Infinito' – 'Così tra questa / Immensità
s'annega il pensier mio: / E il naufragar m'è dolce in questo mare
('Within / this immensity my thinking drowns / and sweet to
me is the sinking in this sea') – as does *Allegria di Naufragi* (The
Joy of Shipwrecks). The 'sovrumani / Silenzi' ('more than human
/ Silences') of Leopardi's poem is indebted in turn to Dante's
neologism 'trasumanar' in Paradiso (1, line 70), 'to pass beyond
the human.' In Dante, paradise requires a new language. For
Ungaretti, his own experience, most intensely his experience of
war, required a new language, words wrested out of silence, and
with abyssal ramifications:

When I discover
in this my silence
a word
it digs into my life
like an abyss
('Poetry,' p. 74)

The experience of war is the central fact of *Il Porto Sepolto*. Of the pressure placed on the poems by the experience, Ungaretti wrote:

> there is will to express, necessity to express, that almost savage exaltation of the *élan vital*, of the appetite for life, which is multiplied by the proximity and daily presence of death.

Ungaretti's war poetry shows little anxiety about the appropriateness of a poem to the predicament. Poetry is accepted, celebrated even, for its tremulous power to offer 'succour / to the man present at his own / fragility' ('Soldier,' p. 46). This is not, therefore, only the poetry of witness, and it is that, and powerfully, but also a poetry where articulation is an end in itself, and one of the characteristics is the poet's ecstatic, if devastated, presence at the achievement of that articulation.

In 1959 Ungaretti visited Japan at last, and in an interview with Okuno Takuya revealed a mellowed response to the comparison of his work with Japanese poetry, admitting an 'affinity,' particularly in those early short poems concerned with the infinite. That Ungaretti's practice in *Il Porto Sepolto* calls to mind Japanese poetry renews our awareness of what that poetry sought, and indeed all poetry seeks, to achieve. In an interview in 1965, Ungaretti, speaking of the poems in this small volume, recalled his awakening to poetry in terms of the effect of war, in which we can also overhear something of Japan:

> War suddenly revealed Language to me. That which I had to say quickly because I might not have enough time to finish, and in the most tragic way ... I had to quickly say what I felt and so if I had to say it quickly, I had to say it with few words, and if I had to say it with few words I had to use words with an extraordinary intensity of meaning.

A Note on the Title

In 1910, the Frenchman, Gaston Nondet, Chief Engineer of Ports and Lights in Egypt, while working on a project to enlarge the western port of Alexandria, came upon an ancient, possibly prehistoric, port structure. His school friends in Alexandria, Jean and Henri Thuile, were the first to bring this to Ungaretti's attention:

> They spoke to me of a port, a submerged port, that must have preceded the Ptolemies, proving that Alexandria was a port even before Alexander. Nothing is known about it.... No other sign remains but that port kept by the sea's depths, the only document handed down through all the ages of Alexandria. The title of my first book derived from that port: *Il Porto Sepolto*.

The obvious, most literal, translation of *Il Porto Sepolto* is *The Buried Port*, but that rendering fails, I think, to capture the sense given to the title by Ungaretti's explication of the meaning the image took on for him:

> the reason this port became the symbol of my poetry is easy to explain. There is in us a secret, the poet dives into the port, discovering this secret, and so comes to give that little a man can give of consolation to his soul.

I hope the rendering here, *The Sunken Keep*, captures at least some of this quality of a secret possessed and maintained, and of its potential re-emergence. Beating behind it is also, perhaps, a memory of Robert Frost's comment on the conflicting interpretations of his poem 'Mending Wall': 'The secret of what it means I keep.' The Italian title carries a 'rhyme' between 'porto' and 'sepolto'. It could be argued that '*bur*ied har*bour*' captures something of this music but English, it seems to me, prefers 'sunken' rather than 'buried' to refer to cities lost to the sea, as in the 2016 exhibition at the British Museum, *Sunken Cities: Egypt's Lost Worlds*. I attempted to capture something of Ungaretti's sound values with 'sunken' and 'keep,' even at the risk of moving away from 'port' and more towards the sense of 'keep' as in castle 'keep.' The military connotation, perhaps, is not out of place, given the circumstances in which the book was written.

ANDREW FITZSIMONS
Tokyo, 2 June 2017

The Sunken Keep

In memory
of
Mohammed Sceab
descendant
of nomad emirs
a suicide
for loss of
a homeland

A lover of France
who became
Marcel
but not French
who no longer knew how
to dwell
in the tent of his kin
to listen to the chant
of the Koran
over coffee

Who could not
give voice
to the song
of his own desolation

I escorted him
with the landlady of the place
where we lodged
in Paris
from 5 Rue des Carmes
a rundown sloping alley

He rests
in the cemetery at Ivry
a suburb locked
forever
in the day a fair
packs up and leaves

Maybe I alone
still know he
lived

And I will
until my turn
to die

Locvizza, 30 September 1916

THE SUNKEN KEEP

The poet emerges
comes to light with song
gives to the wind

Of this poetry
what keeps
is the nullness
of a bottomless secret.

Mariano, 29 June 1916

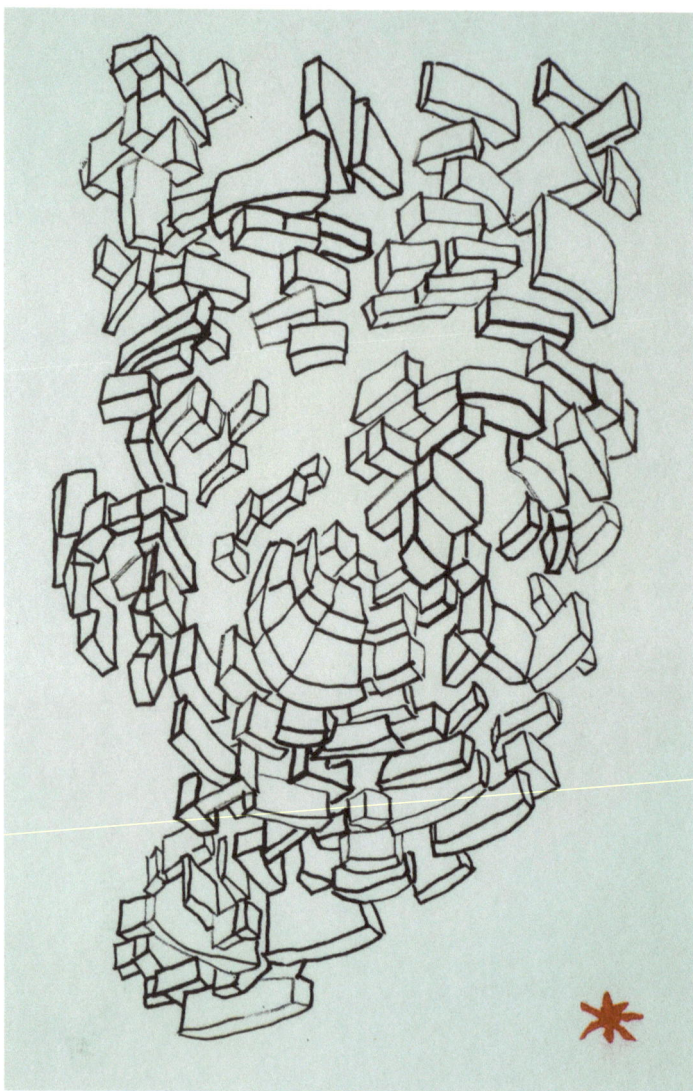

The vanishing plumes of the morning mist
break the silence of the eyes

The wind nibbles the coral
with a thirst of kisses

I whiten with the sun's rise

Life oozes from me
in a meander of nostalgias

I mirror now the points in the world
where I've had friends
and nose out my bearings

Till death in thrall to the journey

We have the respite of sleep

The sun drinks up our tears

I sheath myself in a light mantle
of goldlinen

From this shelf of desolation
I reach to embrace
the good time

Peak 4, 22 December 1915

VIGIL

A full night
flung beside
a butchered
comrade
his lipless
mouth
facing the full moon
his clenched
hands
tearing
my silence
I have written
letters full of love

I have never been
so bound
to life

Peak 4, 23 December 1915

Who will come with me through the fields

The sun sparkles in diamond
waterbeads
on the dewbent grass

I remain pliant
to the inclinations
of the unhurried universe

The mountains dilate
in surges of lilac shadow
and flow with the sky

The spell breaks at that faint vault
and I plunge into myself

Hide in my lair

Versa, 27 April 1916

In the tender round of a smile
we feel twinned to the loosening
of buds of desire

We exhaust ourselves
in the sun's harvest

We beguile ourselves within endless webs
of promises
irradiated with sun

The eyes close
to catch a sweet vanished time
swimming in a lake

We will come to walk the earth again
with this body
grown now too heavy for us

Versa, 27 April 1916

ANNIHILATION

The heart has lavished fireflies
has flashed and sputtered out
from green to green
I have stuttered

With my hands I mould this clay
cricket-thronged
I modulate
this reedy
equally muffled
heart

Loves me loves me not
I am glazed
with pearls
I am rooted
in scorched earth
I have grown
like a berry
on the wrong stem
I have gathered myself
in the freefall
of the star-thistle

Today
like the Isonzo's
deep blue asphalt
I am set
in the grains of the shingle
singled out by the sun
and I transpass
into a flight of clouds

Replete finally
set loose
that child forever daunted
no longer marks time with the heart
has neither time nor place
is content

On my lips I feel
the kiss of marble

Versa, 20 May 1916

SUNSET

The fleshtoned sky
awakens oases
in the nomad of love

Versa, 21 *May* 1916

Breezeblown balustrade
to take the weight of my melancholy
this evening

Versa, 22 May 1916

PHASE

Walk walk
I have re-found
the wellspring of love

In the eye
of a thousand and one nights
I have lain

In the abandoned gardens
I have alighted
like a dove

In the swoon
of the morning
air
I have gathered
oranges and jasmines

Mariano, 25 June 1916

SILENCE

I know a city
which the sun fills every day
and everything is rapt in that moment

I left there one evening
and from the deck
painted white relentless as a squeak

the awaygoing light of solitude

with at its heart a cicada's urgent screech
tearing the tree with its frenzy
with the fresh mirage of its rubied
diadem in the sun

I saw
my city fade
leaving
a while
in the turbid air a lighted kiss
suspended

Mariano, 25 June 1916

WEIGHT

That country soldier
puts faith in
the St Anthony medal
he wears around his neck
and so goes lightly
but alone and naked
unillusioned
I carry my soul

Mariano, 29 June 1916

DAMNATION

Enclosed within mortal things
(the starry sky too will end)
why go for God?

Mariano, 29 June 1916

REEVILLE

My every moment
I've lived
some time else
in a sunken epoch
outside of me

I am faraway with my melancholy
trailing those lost other lives

I come to in a bath
of dear habitual things
surprised
sweetened

The clouds pass
sweetly loosen
to watchful eyes

And I recall
friends
now dead

What is God

And the frightened
creature
opens eyes wide
and gathers in

star drops
the silent plain
and feels
re-given

Mariano, 29 June 1916

MELANCHOLY

Waning melancholy for the body in thrall to destiny

Waning nocturnal abandon
of bodies full-souled
taken
into the vast silence
that eyes do not watch
the apprehension
within this clock
the heart

Sweet abandon
of bodies
heavy with weeping
kiss-shaped
lips
far-off
voluptuousness of bodies
insatiable desires departed

World
Twining spiral of rockets
like a lover's passion
the astonishment of a thousand eyes
in a caravan
of burning pupils

In an evanescent journey
like life that goes from us
in sleep
and the next day recommences
and if it meets death
sleeps only
a little longer

Hill 141, 10 *July* 1916

DESTINY

Faces in torment
like every other
Godmade fibre
why lament?

Mariano, 14 *July* 1916

WHY?

My dark frittered heart
craves relief

Like a blade of this grass
through these mudcaked stones
it wants to tremble slowly toward the light

But I am like
these wormeaten stones
in the catapult of time
like the pebble hurled
on the sharp path of war

From when I gazed
into the world's
immortal face
this child sought knowing
tumbling
into the maze
of the troubled heart

As levelled
as a rail track
my heart's auscultation
yet was found by following
as from its wake
a lost searoute

I watch the horizon
darkening with craters

My heart wants to be lighted
like this night lit
with rocketflare

I bear a heart
that encraters
and thunders and blasts
like a shell
upon the open plain
but leaves in the air
not even the silktrail of flight
My poor heart
clouded
with unknowing

Carsia Giulia, 23 November 1916

SOLDIER

What regiment names you
brothers?

Brother
word trembling
in the night
like a leaf
barely born
a salute
grieving
in the festering air
imploring
whispering
of succour
to the man present at his own
fragility

Mariano, 15 *July* 1916

ONCE UPON A TIME

Bosco Capuccio
has a green velvet
slope
like a sweet
easychair

I doze there
alone
in a remote café
in a pale light
like this
this moon

Hill 141, 1 *August* 1916

I AM A CREATURE

Like this stone
of San Michele
as cold
as hard
as dry
as unyielding
as completely
unsouled
like this stone
my tears
unseen

Death
paid off
living

Valloncello di Cima 4, 5 *August* 1916

I attend the violent night

The air is pocked
like lace
from the gunfire
of men
hidden
in trenches
like snails in shells

It's like
a crazed
troop of chisels
tapping the lava
paving stones
of my streets
and I listen
unseeing
in sleepwake

Valloncello di Cima 4, 6 August 1916

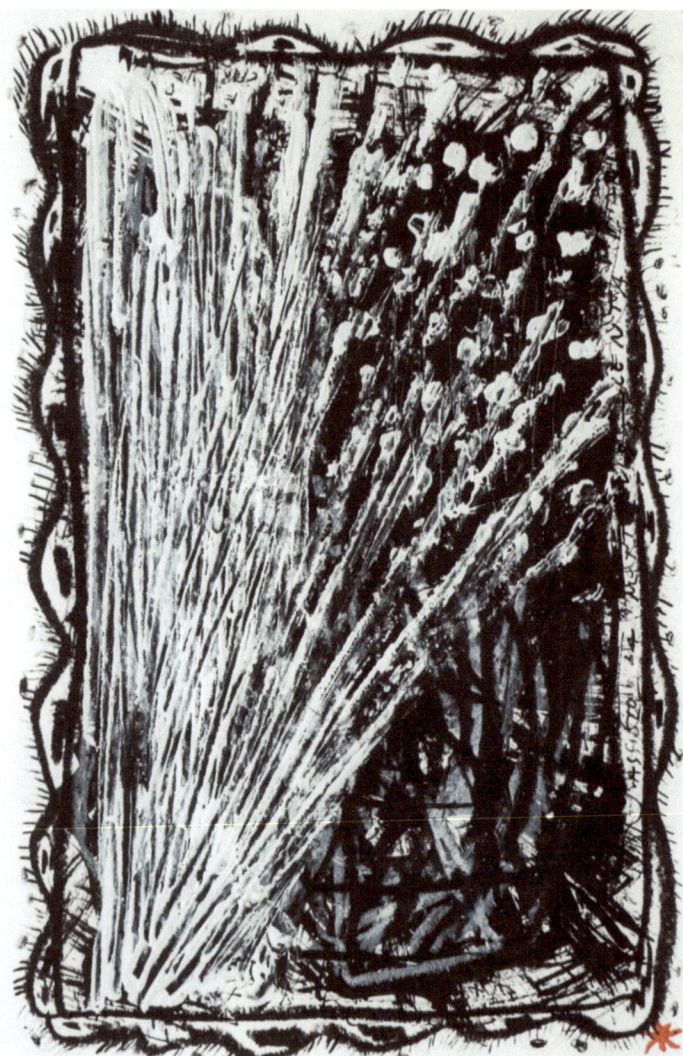

RIVERS

I cling to this mutilated tree
abandoned here in this shellhole
that has the torpor
of a circus
before or after the show
and I watch
the quiet steps
of clouds across the moon

This morning I laid myself
in an urn of water
and like a relic
I reposed

The Isonzo's flow
scrubbed me
like one of its stones

My four limbs
I hauled out and
went off like an acrobat
of the water

I crouched
by my clothes
warfouled
and like a Bedouin
I bowed
to receive
the sun

This is the Isonzo
and here I best
recognised myself
a pliant fibre
of the universe

My torment
comes when
I do not see
myself in harmony

But these unseen
hands
that work me
bequeath me
the rarest
joy

I have re-lived
my life's
stages

These are
my rivers
this the Serchio
from which
two thousand years
or so
of my people's
people

have drawn
and my father and my mother
and this the Nile
that saw me
born and grow
and burn in ignorance
on the vast blue-domed
plains
and this the Seine
in whose turbid flow
I stirred
and came to know myself

These are my rivers
tallied in the Isonzo
and this my nostalgia
that in each of them
I glow
now that it's night
and my life seems to me
a corolla
of shadows

Cotici, 16 August 1916

LANDSCAPE

Stalling between two rocks
I loaf
under this immense
glaucous sky

The tangle of feelings
takes hold of my blindness

There is nothing
more squalid
than this monotony

There was a time
I didn't know
the banality
of the sky's
disappearance
at evening
and worn out
lay down on my African earth
becalmed
by an arpeggio
lost in the air

Valloncello dell'Albero Isolato, 22 August 1916

PILGRIMAGE

Trapped
in these entrails
of wreckage
hours and hours
I have dragged
my carcass
mudclung
as a shoe sole
as the seeds
of the star-thistle

Ungaretti
man of sorrow
illusion is enough
to give you strength

A searchlight
there
makes a sea
in the fog

Valloncello dell'Albero Isolato, 16 August 1916

What song rose tonight
burying
with the crystalline echo of the heart
the illumination of the sky?

What celebration surges
willingly in the heart?

From now on
secretly
the universe's every moment
will well up in me

I have been
a pool
of darkness

Out here in space
I have suckled
like a new born
the breast

Now I am delicate

I am drunk on the universe

From the sea
I have made
a coffin
of freshness

Devetachi, 24 August 1916

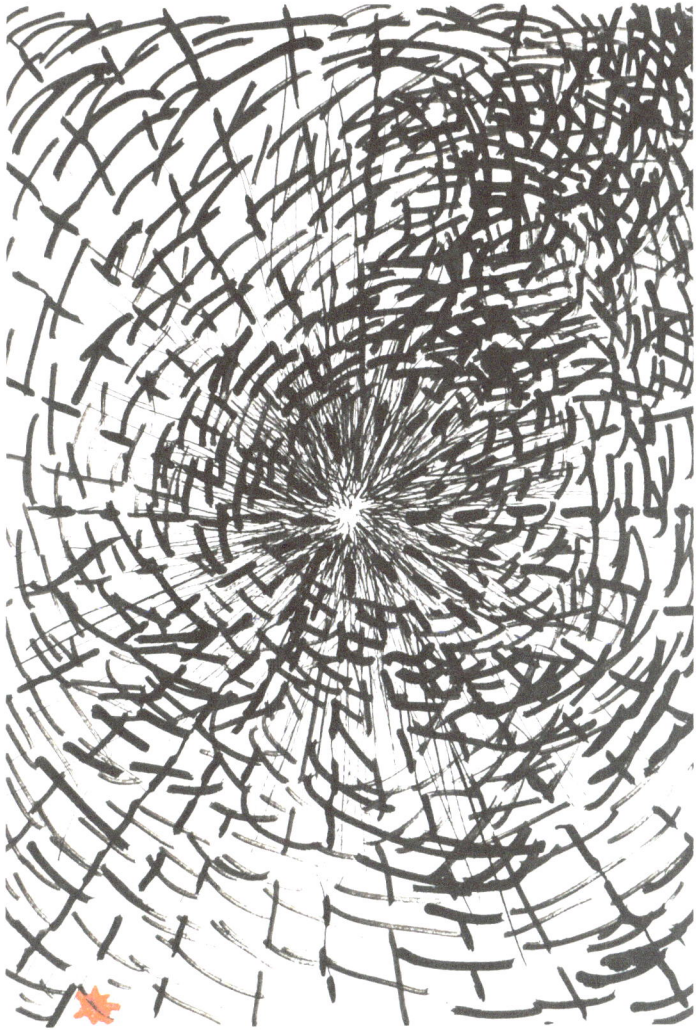

SOMNOLENCE

The mountains' backs
have lain down
in the dark of the valleys

Now there's nothing more
than a throbbing
of crickets
that reaches me

and goes with
my unease

From Devetachi to San Michele, 25 August 1916

SAN MARTINO DEL CARSO

Of these houses
nothing remains
only
ruined wall
exposed to the air

Of all those
who were in touch with me
nothing remains
not even much
in cemeteries

But in the heart
no-one lacks a cross

Raised
as sentinels
to what?

Wounded heart
they are dead

For I see my heart
as a racked country
these times

Valloncello dell'Albero Isolato, 27 August 1916

FRICTION

With my wolflike hunger
I lower
my sheepish body

I am like
a timid boat
on the libidinous ocean.

Locvizza, 23 September 1916

DETACHMENT

Behold a uniformed
man
behold a desert
plain
where the world
makes a mirror

It comes to me I should wake myself
pull myself together
take hold

The rare good born in me
is so slowly born in me
and when it has burned
so imperceptibly
sputters out

Locvizza, 24 September 1916

NOSTALGIA

When the night
is about to disappear
just before spring
and seldom
anyone passes
to get in the way
over Paris gathers
an obscure colour
of tears
that unmakes the buildings
and makes
a mirror
of the slow Seine
with its worn air
of constant distaste
for the touch of lights
in the cranny
of a bridge
I contemplate
the limitless silence
of a girl
flimsy and opaque
as an alpine flower
born from the heart
of a lily of the valley
from the smile of
a canary's
warm corpse
in a desert
noon

and our
maladies
fuse

and like the departed
we remain

Locvizza, 28 *September* 1916

ITALY

I am a poet
a unanimous cry
I am a grume of dreams

I am a fruit
of innumerable grafted hues
ripened in a hothouse

But your people are borne
upon the same land
that bears me
Italy

And in this
your soldier's uniform
I repose
as if it were the cradle
of my father

Locvizza, 1 *October* 1916

Dear
Ettore Serra
poetry
is the world humanity
life itself
flowered from words
the limpid marvel
of a delirious ferment

When I discover
in this my silence
a word
it digs into my life
like an abyss

Locvizza, 2 October 1916

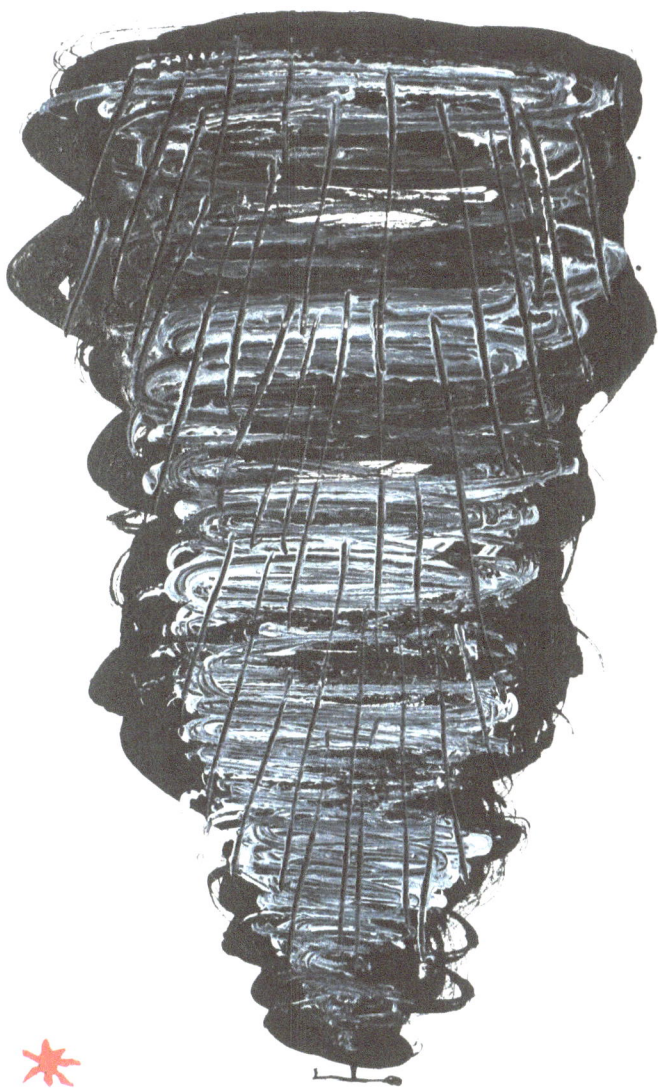

Note: Mohammed Sceab

Muhammad Shihāb, born in Alexandria in 1887, into a family of Lebanese origin, was a schoolfriend of Ungaretti. In 1912 he left Egypt for Paris, where Ungaretti later joined him. He committed suicide on the 9ᵗʰ September 1913.

We were doubly united; we were united in the hope for a more justly organized world, and we were united by the childhood memories and the literary aspirations we both had. Different aspirations: I believed in a poetry where the secret of man … found somehow an echo; I believed in a poetry of the inexpressible. On the other hand, Sceab believed – with his logical mind, an Arab descendant of those who had invented algebra – in a poetry closely linked to reason.

And we had, after all, shared also another drama: we had both had a European education, Western, French. And I too had been born in a country that was not mine, in Alexandria, away from my traditions; away from the landscapes, the images that had accompanied the lives of all of my kin. We were both, for different reasons, men who had not been initiated into life naturally, in a way to fulfill their destinies. And, of course, these things don't happen in a human being without disturbance and without pain, terrible at times. And my, our, youth, our 'first of youth', my own and that of Sceab, is sprinkled with young people, young comrades in the same circumstances as us, who cut their lives short. And Sceab too, at a certain point, cut his life short. Sceab in Paris, far from his African earth – or from his Arab earth because though he was raised in Egypt, he was not African, his people had come from Lebanon – having been reworked by a culture and a different tradition, he could not overcome the conflict and he, too, ended his own life.

9 7 8 4 9 0 7 3 5 9 2 2 5